THE GREAT RACE TO NOME

AN ALASKAN ADVENTURE ACROSS THE CURRICULUM

WRITTEN BY KAREN KRUPNICK ■ ILLUSTRATED BY BEV ARMSTRONG

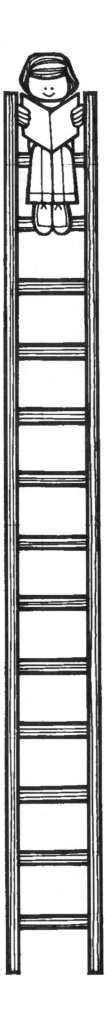

The Learning Works

Cover Design & Illustration:
Bev Armstrong

Text Design and Editorial Production:
Kimberley A. Clark

Acknowledgments

The author would like to thank Sam Hlavaty of the U.S. Sled Dog Sports Federation and the following students for their contributions to this book: Jaime Dietz-Velez, Erin R. Wilson, Jr., Brian Kennedy, and Michael Reisinger.

Copyright © 1995
The Learning Works, Inc.
P.O. Box 6187
Santa Barbara, California 93160

ISBN: 0-88160-246-9

Contents

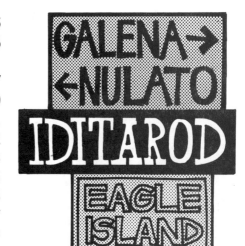

Language Arts Activities

Math Activities

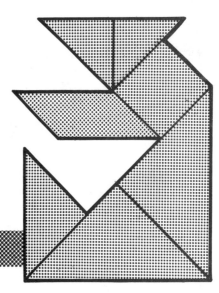

Contents

(continued)

Science Activities

Social Studies and Research Activities

Other Great Race Activities

ataata
ava.
umiaq

Introduction

The Iditarod® Sled Dog Race is a natural for classroom use.* Held annually across more than a thousand miles of Alaskan wilderness, this race contains all of the elements that broadly appeal to children: adventure, excitement, courage, and competition. It is no surprise that a unit based on the Iditarod—a race which celebrates the athletic abilities of both humans and dogs, as well as the relationships between them—is so successful in the classroom.

This book includes activities based on the Iditarod® Sled Dog Race from all areas of the curriculum. They are divided into language arts, math, science, and social studies and research, with activities in art integrated into these areas. The wealth of available literature about the race encourages a strong language-based unit. Critical and creative thinking skills are also emphasized in the activities.

The Iditarod begins on the first Saturday of March, so it is advisable to begin the unit well before that date in order to adequately prepare the students to follow the race. It is helpful to divide the class into groups at the beginning of the unit. Each group can be given several musher biographies to review, and one musher can be selected by the entire group to follow throughout the race. Groups can write cheers, make banners, and write letters of encouragement to their mushers in order to show their support. You can determine the number of activities to pursue in this cooperative learning group situation depending on your needs and classroom environment. Building excitement and enthusiasm before the race begins will enhance the experience for everyone.

The race moves quickly once it begins, so it is essential to get daily updates. Information about how to obtain these updates from the Iditarod Trail Committee is provided in this book. As the race becomes a real-life adventure, students can use the daily updates to plot the mushers' progress on a map of Alaska. Your students will find this an energizing classroom experience, so be prepared to catch "Iditarod Fever."

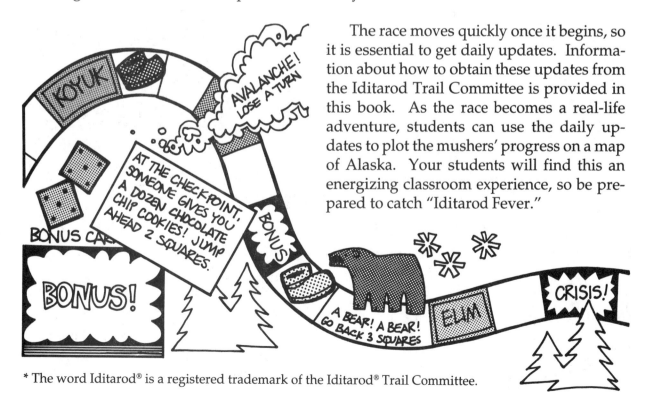

* The word Iditarod® is a registered trademark of the Iditarod® Trail Committee.

The Story of the Iditarod Trail Sled Dog Race

The Iditarod Trail was first used when the Alaskan gold rush began in the 1880s. Towns came alive as gold was discovered. One such town was called Iditarod, named for the Indian word *haiditarod*, which means "a distant place." The Iditarod Trail became a way to reach these distant places. It was full of swamps in the summer, but in the winter it was a major transportation route for the dog sled teams that most people used. It continued to be used until the mid-1920s.

In 1925, an epidemic of **diphtheria** (also called "the Black Death") hit the city of Nome in western Alaska. The disease could be treated with an antitoxin, which was used to fight the bacteria in diphtheria. Unfortunately, the closest antitoxin that could be found was in Anchorage, on the other side of Alaska. Airplanes were still very new, and only flew during the short summer. It was agreed that the medicine would be taken to Nenana by train, and then a relay of dog sled teams would carry it to Nome.

The trip covered almost 700 miles, about two-thirds of which followed the Iditarod Trail. Leonhard Seppala, a Norwegian who had come to Alaska looking for gold, traveled 260 of those miles. He and his lead dog, Togo, crossed the frozen Norton Bay in order to speed the journey. He had to depend on Togo's sense of direction in the blinding snow, and Togo turned out to be a dependable guide. The 260-mile leg that Seppala and his dogs traveled was nearly five times the distance covered by the other teams. The last leg of the run was done by Gunnar Kaason, who had been driving dog teams in Alaska for 21 years. His lead dog was Balto. Balto also proved to be an excellent leader. At one point he refused to go any further and saved the team from falling into icy water. He led the team through blowing snow into Nome, and the diphtheria outbreak was stopped. Balto became a hero. A statue was built in New York's Central Park to honor Balto for his life-saving contributions.

In 1967, a dog sled driver named Joe Redington, Sr. joined with Dorothy Page, an Alaskan interested in her state's history, to celebrate the history and importance of dog sleds. At that time, sleds were being replaced by snowmobiles in Alaska. Redington and Page started an annual sled dog race. In 1973, the course was extended to Nome, with part of it following the old Iditarod Trail. The trip from Anchorage to Nome was similar to the famous diphtheria run of 1925. The race was called the "The Last Great Race on Earth," and Joe Redington and Dorothy Page became known as the "father and mother of the Iditarod."

The Iditarod Trail Committee,
Map of the Iditarod Trail

The Iditarod Trail Committee is the governing body for the race. The committee monitors and updates the rules, requirements, and trail logistics that make the race a reality. With the assistance of a large group of volunteers, the committee makes sure that everything is in place for both humans and dogs when the teams leave the starting line in Anchorage.

The Iditarod Trail Committee also provides an excellent teacher resource packet each year for a nominal fee. The packet contains updates about the race rules, biographies of the mushers for each year's race, updated prize amounts, and a wealth of statistics and interesting facts about the race. This packet can be obtained by contacting:

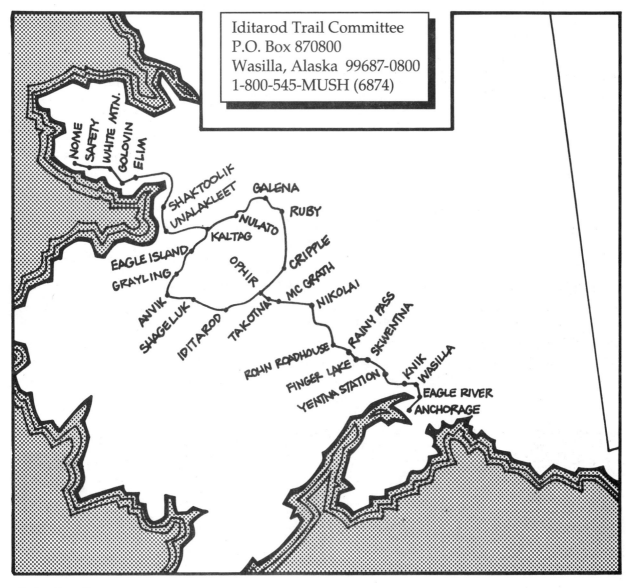

Iditarod Trail Committee
P.O. Box 870800
Wasilla, Alaska 99687-0800
1-800-545-MUSH (6874)

Description of the Iditarod Trail

The Iditarod Race follows two different trails, one in even-numbered years and one in odd-numbered years. The first 13 checkpoints are the same in all years.

1. **Anchorage**
   Population: 190,090. This is Alaska's largest city. The race begins in the center of town on Fourth Avenue where crowds of people come to watch the start.

2. **Eagle River**
   Population: 24,852. The mushers unharness their teams here and truck them to the next checkpoint for the restart.

3. **Wasilla**
   Population: 4,028. The race restarts here.

4. **Knik**
   Population: 272. This is the last checkpoint before entering remote Alaska.

5. **Yentna Station**
   Population: 7. The checkpoint is at the Gabryzack family home.

6. **Skwentna**
   Population: 114. The checkpoint is at the log house of Joe and Norma Delia.

7. **Finger Lake**
   Population: 2. This area is known for its deep snow.

8. **Rainy Pass**
   Population: 2. The highest point on the Iditarod trail, Rainy Pass is in the Alaska Range.

9. **Rohn Roadhouse**
   Population: 0. This area is known for its spectacular scenery. After this checkpoint, mushers go through the famous "Farewell Burn," an area with little snow, but one which is difficult to cross due to tree stumps left as a result of a 1976 fire.

10. **Nikolai**
    Population: 109. This is the first native village on the trail.

11. **McGrath**
    Population: 528. This is the largest settlement in the area.

12. **Takotna**
    Population: 38. This little town has only a store, a restaurant, and a bar, but it is known for its warm welcome for mushers.

13. **Ophir**
    Population: 0. Once a gold rush town, Ophir is now a ghost town.

Description of the Iditarod Trail
(continued)

In even-numbered years, the trail continues to these checkpoints:

14. Cripple

Population: 0. The first musher to reach this halfway mark on the northern route wins $3,000.

15. Ruby

Population: 223. This is the first checkpoint on the Yukon River.

16. Galena

Population: 947. Galena is an Athabascan village.

17. Nulato

Population: 368. An Athabascan village, Nulato was once a Russian trading post.

18. Kaltag

Population: 240. This Athabascan village is where the northern and southern routes join.

19. Unalakleet

Population: 714. This is an Inupiat Eskimo town on the coast of Norton Sound.

20. Shaktoolik

Population: 178. This is one of the windiest stretches of the trail. After this checkpoint, the trail goes across the ice of Norton Bay.

21. Elim

Population: 264. This, like the following two checkpoints, is an Eskimo settlement.

22. Golovin

Population: 127.

23. White Mountain

Population: 180. An eight-hour stop is required here.

24. Safety

Population: 0. Located on the coast of the Bering Sea, this is the last checkpoint before Nome.

25. Nome

Population: 3,500. Nome was once a booming gold rush town. Large crowds turn out to watch the Iditarod finishers come under the famous arch.

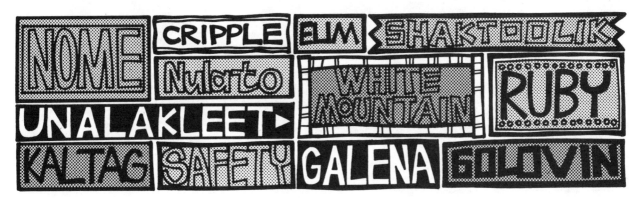

Description of the Iditarod Trail
(continued)

In odd-numbered years, the checkpoints from Ophir to Kaltag are:

14. Iditarod

Population: 0. Once a gold rush community, this is now a ghost town. It is the town from which the original Iditarod Trail took its name. It is the halfway point in odd-numbered years.

15. Shageluk

Population: 139. The name of this town is an Ingalik Indian name which means "village of the dog people."

16. Anvik

Population: 82. This is the first checkpoint on the Yukon River.

17. Grayling

Population: 208. This is the last village checkpoint before Kaltag.

18. Eagle Island

Population: 0. The cabin that is the checkpoint is the only dwelling in the town.

After Eagle Island, the trail joins the northern route at Kaltag.

Race Information and Rules*

The Iditarod Trail Committee updates the rules of the race each year. Changes are made whenever they become necessary. Here is a summary of the rules of the race:

Pre-race Procedure:

1. All participants must be registered by December 1st of the year preceding the race.
2. All mushers must be at least 18 years old at the start of the race.
3. All mushers must pay an entry fee.
4. Food must be sent to the checkpoints before the race.
5. Dogs must be examined before the race by a race veterinarian.
6. Dogs must be "northern breeds" suited for Arctic travel.
7. Dogs must be electronically tagged before the race.
8. Dogs may be dropped during the race, but no dogs may be added to a team.

Rules of the Race:

1. Beginning at 9:00 A.M. on the first Saturday in March, mushers start the race at two-minute intervals. The extra time of these intervals evens out at the checkpoint where the mushers take a mandatory 24-hour layover.
2. Each musher must stop at each checkpoint.
3. Each musher must make a 24-hour stop during the race.
4. Each musher must carry the following items: a sleeping bag, an axe, a pair of snowshoes, eight booties for each dog in the team, one cooker, a notebook to show to the veterinarian at each checkpoint, and promotional materials provided by the Iditarod Trail Committee.
5. A musher will be disqualified for cruel or inhumane treatment of dogs or for improper dog care.
6. No drugs may be used by a musher or given to a dog.
7. A musher will be disqualified if he or she accepts assistance between checkpoints.
8. A musher must allow another musher to pass if he or she comes within 50 feet and asks to pass. This rule does not apply in the last stretch of the race, known as "No Man's Land."
9. There must be only one musher to a team.
10. Each musher must make an eight-hour stop on the Yukon River
11. Each musher must make an eight-hour stop at White Mountain.
12. A musher may have no more than 20 dogs and no fewer than 12 dogs at the start of the race. He or she must have at least five dogs on the line to finish the race.

* Provided courtesy of the Iditarod® Trail Committee.

What Is a Musher?

Someone who drives, or "mushes," a dog team is known as a **musher**. The word probably comes from the French word "marcher," which means "to walk." Long-distance competitive mushing takes great endurance and training for both the human and the dogs in the team. Mushers must spend many hours on the trail in order to be prepared for the difficult job of running such a long race. Since the race goes through many different types of terrain, the musher must train his or her dogs in a variety of settings.

Mushers have their own ideas about how to run the race. Each one must decide how many miles to run on a given day, when to run, what to eat while on the trail, and the best places to stop and rest. Since time is an important part of any race, most mushers do not get very much sleep while on the trail. It is essential for the musher to train in order to keep alert in spite of the lack of sleep, since there are many potential dangers in the wilderness, such as wild animal attacks or blinding snow storms. Decisions must also be made about dog care in order for the dogs to run well and maintain good health. Since it is impossible to predict what might happen while running the race, the members of the team, both human and canine, must be able to rely on each other in order to survive.

Most of the Iditarod® Sled Dog Race mushers live in Alaska, and many live in the area known as the "bush," far from the cities. A few are professional mushers and actually earn a living from racing dog sled teams, but many have other jobs and must train around their busy schedules.

Musher Record Sheet

Daily Musher updates can be obtained during the Iditarod by calling
the Iditarod Hot Line: (907) 248–MUSH.

Musher's Name _____

Date	Checkpoint	Place in Race	Number of Dogs	Miles Traveled	Miles Remaining

Musher Biographies

Joe Redington, Sr.

Joe Redington moved to Alaska in 1948 to mush dogs. He helped to create the Iditarod Trail Sled Dog Race and is known as "The Father of the Iditarod." He has run many Iditarod races himself, as well as the John Beargrease, the Kusko 300, the Knik 200, the Anchorage Fur Rendezvous, and the Alpirod. He and Susan Butcher were the first people to mush dogs to the top of Mt. McKinley. He and his wife run a kennel of sled dogs, and several of their children are also mushers.

Susan Butcher

Susan Butcher moved to Alaska in 1975. She met Joe Redington, Sr. in 1977, and began training with him. In 1979, she and Redington took a dog team to the top of Mt. McKinley. She ran her first Iditarod race in 1976 and has won the race four times. She is known for her outstanding dog care and her love of animals. She and her husband, who is also a musher, live near Fairbanks.

Rick Swenson

Rick Swenson began mushing in Minnesota and moved to Alaska in 1973. He ran his first Iditarod race in 1976 and has run every race since then. He won his first race in 1977, and in 1991 he became the only musher to win the Iditarod five times. He has finished in the top 10 in every Iditarod that he has run.

Musher Biographies
(continued)

Libby Riddles

Libby Riddles began mushing in 1979 and ran her first Iditarod in 1980. She trained her dogs near the Bering Sea, which is a particularly cold and windy part of the Iditarod Trail. This experience helped in 1985, when she became the first woman to win the Iditarod. She did this by going out into a storm along the Bering Sea, while the other mushers waited for the storm to let up.

Martin Buser

Martin Buser is from Switzerland. He came to Alaska in 1979 to learn more about sled dog care, and he ran his first Iditarod in 1980. He won the race in 1992 with a record-breaking time of 10 days, 19 hours, and 17 minutes. His second win in 1994 broke the record again. He and his wife have two children, Nikolai and Rohn, who are both named for checkpoints on the Iditarod trail.

Mary Shields

Mary Shields fell in love with Alaska when she first came to work as a camp counselor in 1965. She moved there shortly after and learned the joys of dog mushing. In 1974, she became the first woman to complete the Iditarod, finishing in 22nd place. She now lives near Fairbanks with her husband and her dogs. She has written several books for children and adults.

What is a Sled Dog?

It is believed that the first Eskimos in Alaska brought dogs and sleds with them from Asia. These dogs were used extensively for hauling materials for the native population. Their use continued in Alaska through the gold rush era, when dog sleds were used to carry gold, mining equipment, and other supplies. Because these were such heavy loads, large, strong dogs such as Alaskan malamutes were used. The malamute is a northern breed that was probably bred from wolves by the Malamute Eskimos.

Malamutes, although ideal sled dogs, were limited in number, so people began breeding them with other types of more common dogs. This created the dogs known as "huskies." In the 1900s, a husky variety that had come from Russia, known as the Siberian Husky, became the commonly accepted sled dog. As racing gained popularity, the search for the perfect racing sled dog continued, and different breeds were introduced. Long-distance racing dogs weigh from 45 to 55 pounds, and must have tough feet, endurance, a willingness to please, and a strong desire to run. Many combinations have been tried in the search for the perfect dog.

The Iditarod® race rules state that the dogs used in the race must be "northern breeds." These dogs generally have been bred for many years to work on the trail, and sledding is natural for them. The dogs known as Alaskan huskies are common among racing dogs, and often these are mixtures of many breeds of dogs. Huskies can travel as fast as 20 miles an hour. Dogs today can run faster than their ancestors because they are fed and trained differently. They are bred more carefully for certain characteristics. Many mushers have strong opinions about the perfect diet for their dogs. The care given by a musher can make a great deal of difference in how that musher's dogs will run.

Training the Dogs

Sled dogs that run in long-distance races need rigorous training like any other athlete. It is recommended that any dog that will be running a 1,000-mile race should have a minimum of 1,500 miles of training spread over at least a six-month period. Dogs need to train under the same conditions they will be facing in the race, so they must practice pulling a heavy sled or running for several hours at a time. Weather conditions along the Iditarod trail can be very harsh, so dogs need to be accustomed to severe cold and wind.

Mushers are aware that dogs can develop frostbite in areas of their bodies that are less protected than others, so sometimes these parts of their bodies are covered. Their feet are also in need of protection from the hazards of the trail, and booties are used to protect them. In addition, dogs—just like humans—can become dehydrated on the trail and need to drink water frequently.

There are some basic commands that the dogs must know on the trail. "Gee" means right turn, "haw" means left turn, and "come gee" and "come haw" are instructions for making a full turn in either direction. If a musher wants the team to go, the command is "mush," "hike," "all right," or "let's go!" A command to stop is "whoa!" Each dog must be ready to listen to and obey these commands in order to be a valuable member of a sled dog team.

The size of the team varies according to the pulling strength necessary for each situation. The Iditarod race rules state that a team can start with at least 12 and no more than 20 dogs. Mushers can leave dogs at pick-up points along the way if they are injured or no longer needed, but there must be at least five dogs in the team when the musher crosses the finish line in Nome.

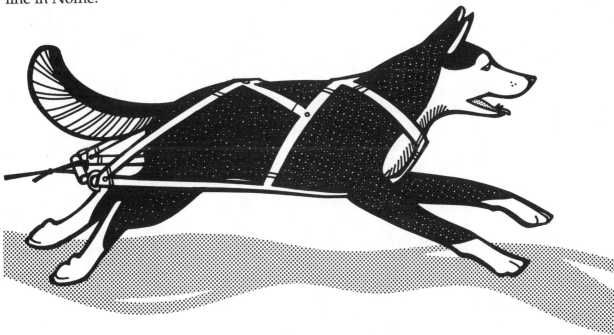

All About Sleds

The original dog sleds, used by Eskimos about 1,500 years ago, were made of bones that were tied together with leather thongs. The **runners**, the parts that slide along the snow, were made of walrus ivory. Today's Iditarod sled is quite different from that original design. It is now an efficient racing machine as well as a means of transportation.

The sled used for long-distance races like the Iditarod is known as a **toboggan** sled. It is built close to the ground and does not tip over easily. The sled has a large basket which allows it to carry the gear necessary for a long race. It weighs between 45 and 50 pounds, and is about six feet long.

The major parts of the sled are:

basket   The basket is the part of the sled that sits over the runners and is used for carrying gear, injured dogs, or anything else that needs to be carried.

brake   The brake is a piece of wood that is attached to the center brace under the basket. It has a steel claw on the end that the musher steps on to stop the sled. It is attached to the sled by a long spring.

bridle   The bridle is a rope that extends from the front two stanchions and under the brushbow. The gangline, which is attached to the dogs, connects to the bridle.

brushbow   The brushbow is a circular projection in front of the sled that acts as a "bumper," since it is the first part of the sled to hit trees, etc. The brushbow must be strong in order to protect the rest of the sled and the musher.

handlebow   Also called the driving bow, this device steers the sled. It is made of wood or plastic and wrapped with rawhide, tape, or nylon string to protect the musher's hands. Twisting the handlebows causes the runners to turn on their edges, which allows the sled to turn more easily.

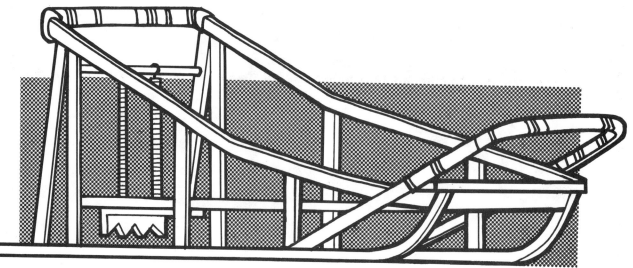

All About Sleds
(continued)

runners   Runners are the bottom part of the sled that slide along the snow. They are usually made of wood and are covered in plastic. Iditarod racers change the runners during the race, depending on the trail conditions.

stanchions   These form the framework of the sled. Sleds can have one, two, or three stanchions. They are attached by bolts or tied with rawhide or nylon strings.

standing pad   This is the part of the sled that the musher stands on. It is behind the last
or foot pad   stanchion and is covered in a slip-resistant material.

There are many things that a musher has to consider when choosing a sled. The runners must be able to slide well across different types of land. The sled must be easy to control while carrying the heavy load required for a long-distance race. The brake must allow the musher to stop suddenly. The sled must be safe and easy to use.

Design a sled that could be used by a doctor, a repair person, a delivery person, a sales-person, an artist, or someone in another occupation. Include all of the features mentioned above. Write a 50-word advertisement for your sled.

_____

_____

_____

_____

Name _____

Great Race Vocabulary

blizzard   a storm with driving snow, strong winds, and intense cold

frostbite   an injury to any part of the body caused by excessive exposure to extreme cold

glacier   a large, slow-moving mass of ice formed over many years from snow which has fallen and accumulated

hypothermia   a condition of dangerously low body temperature

kayak   an Eskimo canoe made of a light framework covered with animal skins and propelled with a double-bladed paddle

malamute   a breed of large dogs with a dense, coarse coat, which was originally raised by Alaskan Eskimos for pulling sleds

parka   a hooded, pullover fur coat, for wear in the Arctic and other cold regions

permafrost   a layer of permanently frozen soil below the surface in polar regions

stamina   the ability to endure disease, fatigue, etc.

taiga   a subarctic evergreen forest that begins where the tundra ends

tundra   a treeless area between the ice cap and the tree line of arctic regions, with mucky, black soil and a permanently frozen subsoil and supporting dense, low-growing vegetation, such as lichens, mosses, and stunted shrubs

Name _____

Mushers' Vocabulary

All right! Let's go! Mush! Hike!	commands to start the team
booties	socks that protect a dog's feet from cuts and sores
Come gee!	command for a full right turn
Come haw!	command for a full left turn
Gee!	command for right turn
Haw!	command for left turn
lead dog	the dog that runs in front of the others on a team
musher	a person who competes in cross-country races with a dog team and sled
swing dog	the dog that runs directly behind the leader of a team
team dog	any dog other than the lead dog, the swing dog, and the wheel dog
tow line	main rope that runs forward from the sled
Trail!	request for right-of-way
tug line	line that connects a dog's harness to the tow line
wheel dog	the dog that is positioned directly in front of the sled
Whoa!	command to halt the team

Name _____

Woodsong
by Gary Paulsen

Gary Paulsen, author of *Hatchet*, has also written books for children and adults about dog sled racing. *Woodsong* is Gary Paulsen's personal account of his training for and running of the Iditarod. Because mushers get so little sleep while running the race, it is common for them to have hallucinations—visions of scenes or objects that do not exist outside the mind. Gary Paulsen describes some of his in this book.

Draw a hallucination that you might have if you were running the Iditarod. Write about it on the lines at the bottom of the page.

_____

_____

_____

_____

_____

_____

Name _____

Black Star, Bright Dawn
by Scott O'Dell

Black Star, Bright Dawn is the story of a young Alaskan native girl who is caught between her father's attachment for the "old ways" and the ways of the new world around her. Her journey toward adulthood takes an unexpected turn when she finds herself about to run the Iditarod Sled Dog Race. Read *Black Star, Bright Dawn* and then complete this activity.

Imagine that you are a reporter for a newspaper and your assignment is to interview Bright Dawn. Write questions that you would ask and the answers you think she might give.

Reporter: _____

_____

Bright Dawn: _____

_____

_____

Reporter: _____

_____

Bright Dawn: _____

_____

_____

Reporter: _____

_____

Bright Dawn: _____

_____

_____

Black Star, Bright Dawn
The Sequel

You have been given the job of writing a sequel for *Black Star, Bright Dawn*.

1. Where will the sequel take place?

2. Summarize the plot in five sentences or less.

3. What will the conclusion be?

4. On a separate sheet of paper, design a book cover for this sequel.

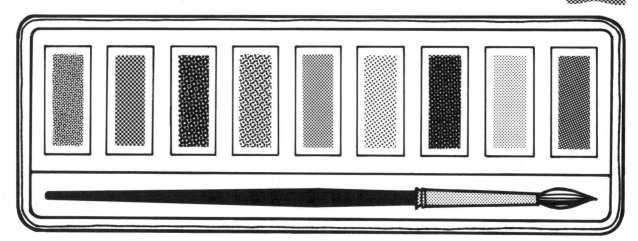

Name _____

Great Race Dictionary

On the lines below, write a word relating to sled dog racing beginning with that particular letter of the alphabet. If you have trouble with some of the less common letters (Q, X, Z), try to think of a word that has that letter anywhere in it. You may include words you know relating to Alaska, such as names, animals, or native words.

A _____   N _____

B _____   O _____

C _____   P _____

D _____   Q _____

E _____   R _____

F _____   S _____

G _____   T _____

H _____   U _____

I _____   V _____

J _____   W _____

K _____   X _____

L _____   Y _____

M _____   Z _____

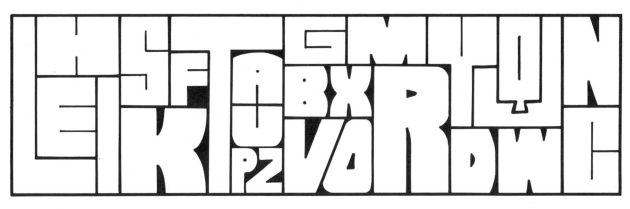

Name _____

Snow Poetry

In the space below, list some of the snowy places you have lived in or visited. Try to think of snowy places that were away from cities or towns. If you have never been in a snowy place, use your imagination to create a frosty scene.

Write down whatever words come to mind when you think of your snowy setting.

Put your words together to create a poem. The lines of your poem do not have to rhyme. Use descriptive words that involve the senses—the sight, sound, and feel of snow.

Name _____

Snow Poetry
Student Samples

Calling Iditarod

It's like being in a sea of wonders.
You are the wild,
calling up to the sky.
White snow is a cushion for you.

Jaime A. Dietz-Velez

The Iditarod

Slicing sleds,
Snow flying.
Dogs running,
Mushers yelling.
That's the Iditarod.

Erin R. Wilson, Jr.

Iditarod

Iditarod, Iditarod
I like you a lot
I wish I could run you
But I'm not old
Enough!

Brian Kennedy

Name _____

What Makes a Good Lead Dog?

Not every dog can be a lead dog. A lead dog must possess certain important characteristics. Do research to find out more about the traits that make a dog suitable to lead a team. Then, in each circle, write a word that could be used to describe a lead dog.

Name _____

My Life as a Lead Dog

Imagine that you are a lead dog. Using the web that you created on page 28, write a story about your life and adventures. In your story, include as many items from the web as you can.

_____

_____

_____

_____

_____

_____

_____

_____

_____

_____

_____

_____

The Great Reading Race Contest

1. Select a book you would like to read and show it to your teacher to obtain his or her approval. On the first night of the Iditarod, begin reading your book. Continue reading each night of the race.

2. Each night, enter the number of pages read on *The Great Reading Race Record Sheet* on page 31 and have an adult sign the entry.

3. Move your pin on a map of Alaska each day to indicate your progress on the trail if the number of pages read were miles. Try to keep up with your musher on the trail.

4. Any student who reaches Nome by the time the last musher (the Red Lantern winner) is in will receive a prize. Students who reach Nome by the time their mushers do will receive special prizes.

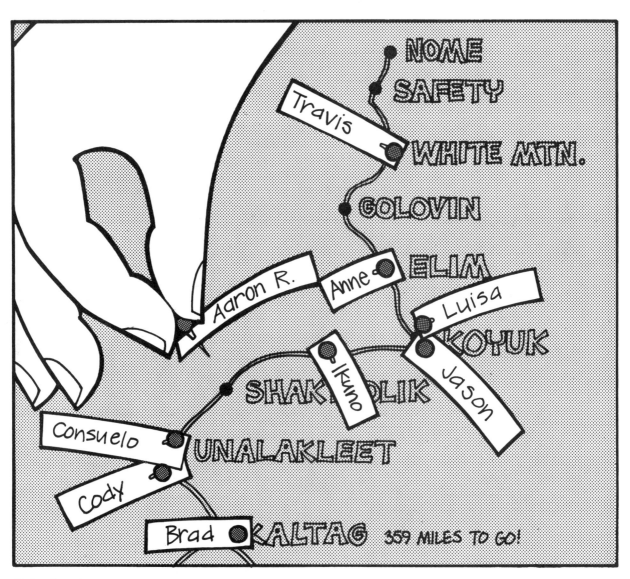

Name _____

The Great Reading Race Record Sheet

Date	Title of Book	Pages Read	Adult's Signature

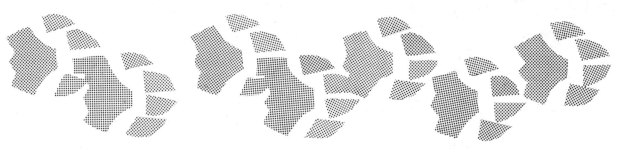

Extended Language Arts Activities

✳ Imagine that you will be a musher in the next Iditarod. Write a short biography about yourself to be printed in the Iditarod brochure.

✳ Write a letter to Bright Dawn congratulating her on her completion of the Iditarod.

✳ Write a song about the Iditarod.

✳ Imagine that you are a sports reporter for your local newspaper. Write an article announcing the upcoming start of the race. Be sure to explain the race thoroughly for those readers who do not know about it.

✳ Imagine that you are a dog in a musher's kennel and you are not chosen to go to the Iditarod. Write a letter telling your musher how you feel.

✳ Read one of the books listed in the bibliography (pages 69–71). Write a book review to inform your classmates about it.

✳ If you were an Iditarod musher, what names would you give to the 20 members of your dog team? Explain why you chose these particular names.

✳ Veterinarians examine the dogs at checkpoints to be sure that they are in good physical condition during the race. Make a list of the things that you would look for if you were a veterinarian and explain why.

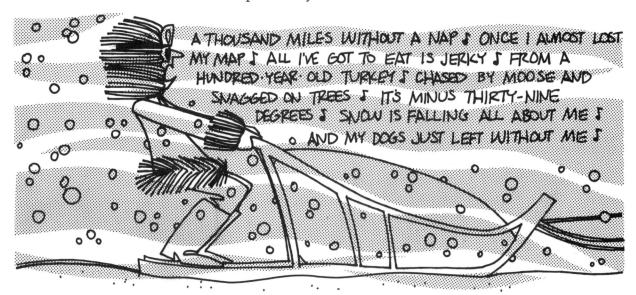

A THOUSAND MILES WITHOUT A NAP ♪ ONCE I ALMOST LOST MY MAP ♪ ALL I'VE GOT TO EAT IS JERKY ♪ FROM A HUNDRED-YEAR OLD TURKEY ♪ CHASED BY MOOSE AND SNAGGED ON TREES ♪ IT'S MINUS THIRTY-NINE DEGREES ♪ SNOW IS FALLING ALL ABOUT ME ♪ AND MY DOGS JUST LEFT WITHOUT ME ♪

Extended Language Arts Activities
(continued)

Super Language Arts Challenge

✳ Imagine that the dogs in the dog yard could talk to each other. Write a play based on the conversation they have the night before the start of the Iditarod.

> ✳ Pretend that you are an Iditarod musher and you collect items along the way as you are racing. Make a scrapbook of the items you collected. Write a description of each item and explain where the items came from.

✳ Create a four-panel comic strip about an imaginary lead dog. Use cartoon "bubbles" to show what the main characters are saying and thinking.

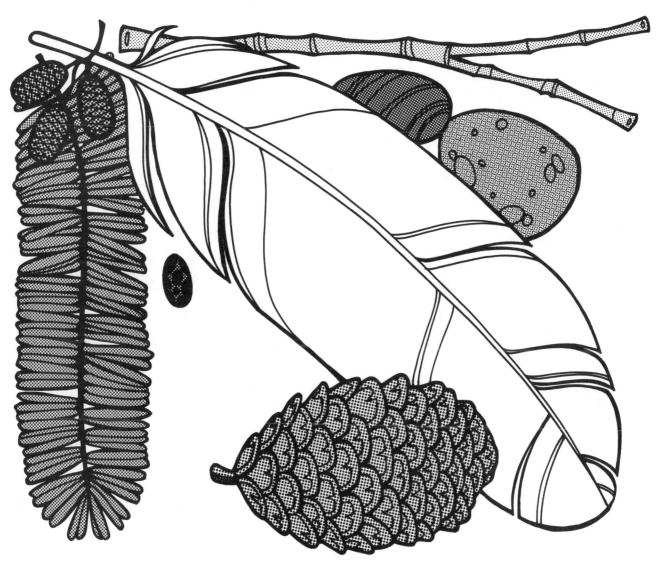

Name _____

Tangrams

Tangrams are Chinese puzzles composed of seven geometric shapes that can be put together in a variety of patterns. The tangram can be arranged in a square, like the one below, or in an endless array of patterns. Trace and cut out the tangram pieces below, and then put them together again to create the Iditarod pictures found on page 35. Have fun arranging them to make tangram pictures of your own.

Name ——————————————

Tangram Designs

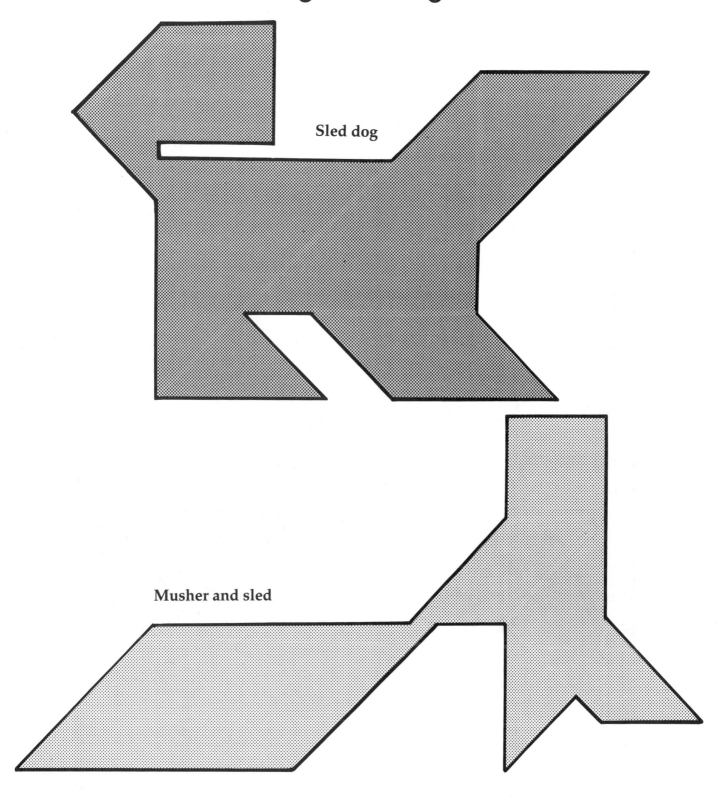

Sled dog

Musher and sled

Musher Card Math

Use the facts on these musher cards to complete the worksheet. Race times shown reflect how long it took the musher to complete the race in days, hours, minutes, and seconds. For example, 15:07:02:47 is 15 days, 7 hours, two minutes, and 47 seconds.

Jeff King

Jeff King

Born in California, Jeff King came to Alaska in 1975 to work at Denali National Park. He now lives near the entrance to the park with his wife and three daughters. He won the 1993 Iditarod race in record time.

Iditarod Race Record:

1981	28th	15:07:02:47	1992	6th	11:10:40:35
1991	12th	13:14:24:40	1993	1st	10:15:38:15

Other Races:

Yukon Quest Winner, 1989
Kusko 300 Winner, 1991–1993

Dee Dee Jonrowe

Dee Dee Jonrowe

Dee Dee Jonrowe was born in Germany while her father was in the army. She moved to Alaska in 1971. She ran her first Iditarod race in 1980.

Iditarod Race Record:

1980	24th	17:07:59:24	1988	9th	13:16:29:06
1981	31st	16:05:05:43	1989	4th	11:13:47:16
1983	15th	13:18:10:25	1990	5th	11:14:41:31
1984	30th	15:19:18:13	1991	7th	13:13:34:10
1987	22nd	13:02:58:15	1992	5th	11:09:05:00
			1993	2nd	10:16:10:50

Other Races:

John Beargrease Sled Dog Marathon Winner, 1989
Alpirod, 1991, 2nd Place
Alpirod, 1993, 3rd Place
Alpirod, 1994, 3rd Place

Name _____

Musher Card Math Worksheet

Use the information on one of the musher cards to complete the following.

1. musher's name _____

2. place of birth _____

3. fastest Iditarod finish time _____ year _____

4. slowest Iditarod finish time _____ year _____

5. What was the difference in time between these two races?

   _____ days _____ hours _____ minutes _____ seconds

6. Using data from all of this musher's completed Iditarod races:

   a. Calculate the *average* place finished. _____

   b. Calculate the *average* number of days needed to complete the
      race. _____

7. On a separate piece of paper write two word problems of your own using
   the information on the musher card. Have a friend solve them.

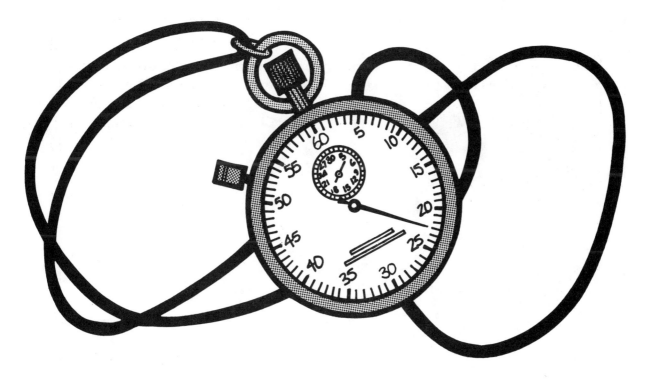

Name _____

Math Challenges

1. It is 18 miles from Anvik to Grayling. Grayling to Eagle Island is 60 miles. How far is it from Anvik to Eagle Island and back again?

2. If Unalakleet has 714 people and Grayling has 208 people, how many more people does Unalakleet have?

3. Anchorage has 190,090 people. Eagle River has 24,852 people. What is the total population of these two cities?

4. Rick Swenson started racing in 1971. How many years has he been racing?

5. Gary Paulsen has 22 sponsors. He loses five and then gets 18 more. How many sponsors does he have?

6. Joe Runyan buys seven dogs at $625 each. What is the total cost for the seven dogs?

7. Rick Swenson has 12 booties for each of his 18 dogs. At McGrath, the checker asked how many booties he had left. He said that he had used two sets of booties (there are four booties in a set) for each dog. How many booties did he have left?

8. It is 1,161 miles from Anchorage to Nome. Susan has traveled 983 miles. How many more miles does she have to travel to reach Nome?

9. If it is 1,161 miles from Anchorage to Nome, and it is 474 miles from Anchorage to Ophir, how many miles is it from Ophir to Nome?

10. The German, Spanish, Japanese, and American film crews each film the Iditarod four times a day. How many times has each crew filmed after 11 days?

More Math Challenges

1. Each of the 13 mushers at Finger Lake checkpoint ate five bowls of soup. Five of them went back for a sixth bowl. How many bowls of soup were eaten?

2. Martin Buser has three dog teams. One team has 18 dogs, the second has one-half that number, and the third has two-thirds that number. How many dogs does he have in all?

3. The first musher at the start in Anchorage leaves the gate at 9:02 A.M., and another musher leaves every two minutes after that. At what time will the 40th musher leave the gate?

4. The temperature in Anchorage on the day the race starts is 16 degrees above zero. It is –36 degrees that day in Nome. What is the difference in temperature between the two cities?

5. The mileage of the northern route is 1,161 miles, and the southern route is 1,163 miles. If an Iditarod musher were to finish the Iditarod race in *exactly* 10 days, how many miles would he or she have to travel each day on each route?

6. Eight mushers left dogs to be picked up at Rainy Pass. The dogs weighed 43 lbs., 62 lbs., 46 lbs., 66 lbs., 50 lbs., 47 lbs., 58 lbs., and 51 lbs. What is the combined weight of the eight dogs? If a plane could carry only 200 lbs. of cargo on each trip, how many trips would it have to make in order to move all the dogs?

7. A minimum of five lbs. of dog food per dog must be sent to all Class A checkpoints, and a minimum of two lbs. per dog must be sent to each Class B checkpoint. If a musher has 16 dogs, what is the minimum amount of food that must be sent to each Class A checkpoint and to each Class B checkpoint?

8. Suppose that each musher must pay $1,750 in entry fees in order to run the Iditarod. If 71 mushers enter the race, how much money is collected in entry fees?

9. A musher trains his team for three hours each day in November and four hours each day in December. How many hours does the team train in these two months?

10. There are 67 mushers running in the Iditarod. If each musher has 18 dogs, and each dog must have at least five lbs. of food per dog at each of the 10 Class A checkpoints, what is the minimum amount of food at each checkpoint? What is the minimum amount of food at all 10 checkpoints combined?

Name _____

Great Race Mind Benders

1. Pretend that the Iditarod Trail Committee has $355,000 in prize money to divide among the first 20 mushers who finish the race. The first-place musher will get $50,000. How would you divide the rest of the prize money among the other 19 mushers? Explain in writing how you arrived at your answer.

2. You have 18 dogs in your team. Three are trained to be lead dogs, and five others are trained to be wheel dogs. You would like to use as many different team arrangements as possible during the race. How many combinations of dogs can you list? Explain your answer.

Name _____

Sleds in Color

Rick Swenson, Susan Butcher, Jeff King, and Martin Buser are driving red, green, blue, and purple sleds. Using the clues below, determine which musher is driving each sled.

Clues:

1. The blue sled is behind Rick's sled and the red sled.
2. Susan shared her hot chocolate with Jeff and the driver of the purple sled.
3. Martin's lead dog is barking at the lead dogs of the purple sled and the red sled.
4. Martin's sled is in front of Susan's sled and the blue sled.

	red	green	blue	purple
Rick Swenson				
Susan Butcher				
Jeff King				
Martin Buser				

Sled Dogs in Line

Granite, Fidget, Mousey, Flopsey, and Jack are sled dogs in the same team. Using the clues below, determine each dog's position.

Clues:

1. Flopsey is between Fidget and Mousey.
2. Neither Jack nor Fidget is the wheel dog.
3. Granite is furthest from the sled.
4. The dog with the shortest name is right behind the lead dog.

	fifth (wheel dog)	fourth (team dog)	third (team dog)	second (swing dog)	first (lead dog)
Fidget					
Flopsey					
Granite					
Jack					
Mousey					

Name _____

Musher Movers

Dee Dee Jonrowe, Susan Butcher, Martin Buser, Jeff King, and Joe Redington, Sr. are each located at one of the following checkpoints: Skwentna, Rainy Pass, Rohn Roadhouse, Nikolai, and McGrath. Which musher is at each checkpoint?

Clues:
1. Both Dee Dee and Martin are past the Farewell Burn.
2. The Father of the Iditarod is at the highest point on the trail.
3. There is a woman in the lead.
4. Jeff is at Joe and Norma Delia's log house.

	Skwentna	Rainy Pass	Rohn Roadhouse	Nikolai	McGrath
Dee Dee Jonrowe					
Susan Butcher					
Martin Buser					
Jeff King					
Joe Redington, Sr.					

Name _____

Extended Math Activities

These activities can be done during the race using information from the daily updates.

- Make a line graph showing the number place of your musher each day.

- Keep a line graph of the temperature on the trail each day.

- Calculate the difference in temperature on the trail and in your town each day.

- Make a line graph of the number of dogs your musher has each day.

- Make a bar graph of the number of miles your musher travels each day.

These activities can be done with information from your papers.

- Calculate the distance between checkpoints. Which two checkpoints are furthest apart? Which two are closest?

- Calculate the distance of the entire race on the northern trail and on the southern trail? What are the totals? Which route is longer?

- Make a bar graph showing the population of the checkpoints.

Name _____

Extended Math Activities
(continued)

Super Math Challenge

- Analyze the bar graph you made showing the population of the checkpoints. Compare the least and most populated. Give reasons for the differences.

- Calculate what time it is in each time zone of the United States when the race begins in Anchorage.

- Each day, calculate the average miles your musher has covered per hour that he or she has been on the trail.

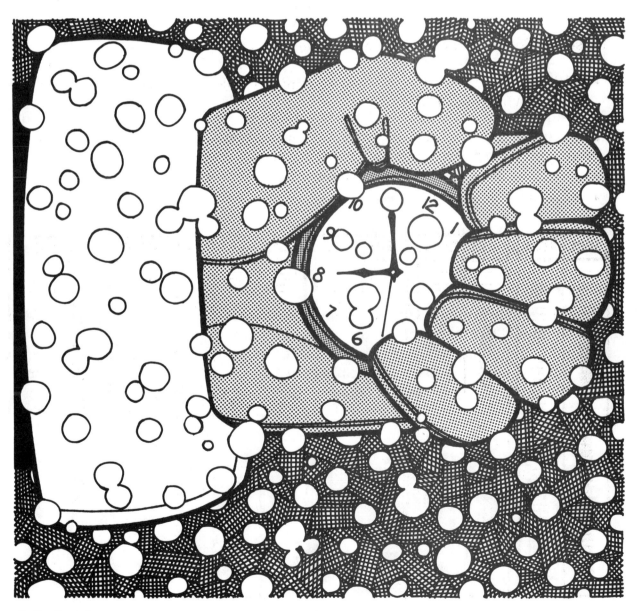

Name _____

Aurora Borealis

The **Aurora Borealis**, or "Northern Lights," originates far away on the sun. Solar winds caused by hot gases from the sun carry electrically charged particles with them. When these particles enter the earth's atmosphere, most enter near the poles, since openings occur in the earth's magnetic fields there.

The magnetic lines of the earth extend from the North Pole to the South Pole. Particles entering the atmosphere get trapped in these lines, where they collide with gas particles. These collisions give off energy that we see as lights.

Most auroras take place near the magnetic poles, but they can occasionally extend to the equator. The particles can bounce back and forth from the North Pole to the South Pole in a few seconds, so auroras can take place at both polar areas at the same time. The Aurora Borealis takes place at the North Pole, while the **Aurora Australis** occurs at the South Pole.

Auroras can take different shapes and forms, and no two are alike. An aurora can take the form of an "arc," and appear as a pale green strip from one horizon to another. This form occurs between 7:00 and 10:00 P.M. Later in the evening, the aurora develops vertical bars of light called "rays," which line up with the earth's magnetic lines. The rays move around in bands, and the color red appears at the bottom and front edge. The midnight aurora is called the **corona**. After midnight, a pale green remains in the sky and patches of light appear that look like puffs of smoke. These patches appear to blink on and off.

The aurora can be seen in Alaska all year except from May to August, when the night sky is too bright. Sometimes it is visible almost every night in the winter. Iditarod racers frequently see the Northern Lights while on the trail.

Just for Fun

You can get a better idea of the lines of magnetism of the earth by using a bar magnet and iron filings. Place the bar magnet on a table with the top facing North. Place a piece of paper over the magnet and carefully sprinkle the filings over the magnet onto the paper. Gently tilt the paper, and you will see the filings line up along the lines of magnetism from the north pole of the magnet to the south pole. The lines they form are similar to the lines connecting the earth's poles. The particles that make up the aurora travel along these lines from pole to pole.

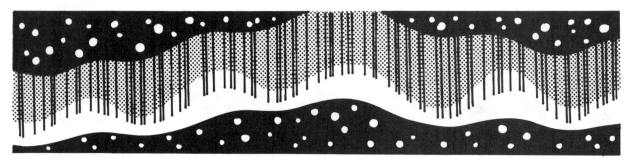

Alaskan Wildlife

Alaskan winters are very harsh. In order to live in such an environment, animals must develop effective adaptations. The following is a list of some Alaskan animals and explanations of how they have adapted in order to survive:

caribou   Caribou are strong swimmers and are able to cross bodies of water in order to move from place to place. Herds migrate in the spring to locations where wind has blown away the snow and food is available. Newborn caribou are able to run almost immediately, which helps keep them safe from predators.

wolf   Wolves travel in packs when food is scarce. They have thick fur to keep them warm in the intense cold.

ptarmigan   Ptarmigan are grouses, or a kind of northern bird. They are camouflaged in both summer and winter. In the summer they are brown to blend into the brush, and in the winter they turn white to blend with the snow. This defense keeps them safe from their many predators.

trumpeter swan   Trumpeter swans are the largest swans in the world. They escape the harsh winter by migrating to Canada or southeastern Alaska. They have long flight feathers to help them make the journey.

polar bear   Polar bears are ideally suited to their environment. They are camouflaged in order to blend into the whiteness around them. They also have extremely thick fur and a layer of fat to keep them warm in extreme cold. The female bear makes a winter den where she and her new cubs stay until the spring.

brown bear   This variety of bear eats all summer in order to fatten itself for the winter. A brown bear finds a den in the fall and spends the whole winter in it. It comes out again in the spring and begins looking for food.

Just for Fun

Compare the characteristics of an arctic animal with a similar animal from a warmer climate. Here are some examples: snowshoe rabbit/jackrabbit, polar bear/black bear, arctic fox/coyote, snowy owl/great horned owl, lemming/kangaroo rat.

Name _____

Extended Science Activities

Aurora Borealis

Look for library books containing photographs of the aurora. Try one or more of the following activities:

- Use the sides of large pieces of pastel chalk to draw a picture of the aurora on black paper.

- Write a story that takes place on a night when the aurora is visible.

- Indian groups of the far north believed that the Northern Lights were torches carried by spirits who were looking for the souls of those who were about to die. Write a legend explaining your ideas about the origin of the aurora.

Other Science Activities

- Alaska has many glaciers. How is a glacier formed? What does a glacier need to exist year after year? Illustrate your findings on a chart.

- In 1964, the biggest earthquake ever recorded in North America shook Alaska. Locate facts about this earthquake and write a brief report.

- Alaska has active volcanoes. Find information about the most recent eruption, and locate the site on a map.

- Imagine that you are an arctic animal. Write a story from the animal's point of view about life in Alaska's harsh climate.

- The plants of Alaska, like the wildlife, are adapted to survive despite the harsh weather conditions and frozen ground. Research at least three of these plants and explain their adaptations.

Name _____

Extended Science Activities
(continued)

Super Science Challenge

- Scientists and NASA recently sent a robot into a live volcano in Alaska to study it in a way that humans could not. Make a list of questions that you would like the robot to answer.

- Imagine that you are an architect and design a home in northern Alaska. What features would you include to safeguard the house from the effects of permafrost and cold?

- In 1989, an oil tanker called the *Exxon Valdez* hit a reef in Prince William Sound causing a massive oil spill. Research the impact of this spill on Alaska's wildlife.

- To illustrate the effect of oil in water, add a few drops of salad oil to a bowl of water. What do you observe? Try to mix the oil into the water. What happens? Relate your observations to the oil spill in Alaska.

Name _____

Alaskan Mapworks

Place the following checkpoints, bodies of water, and mountains in the correct locations on the map of Alaska on page 51.

Alaska Range
Aleutian Islands
Anchorage
Anvik
Arctic Circle
Arctic Ocean
Bering Sea
Brooks Range

Canada
Elim
Fairbanks
Gulf of Alaska
Juneau
Kaltag
Knik

Kodiak Island
Mt. McKinley
Nome
Ophir
Point Barrow
Ruby
Saint Lawrence Island
Shaktoolik

Mount Mc Kinley
BERING SEA
JUNEAU
ALEUTIAN ISLANDS
POINT BARROW
Ophir Elim Kodiak Island
SHAKTOOLIK KNIK ANVIK
ARCTIC CIRCLE Nome FAIRBANKS
Arctic Ocean CANADA
Ruby Anchorage Kaltag

Name _____

Map of Alaska

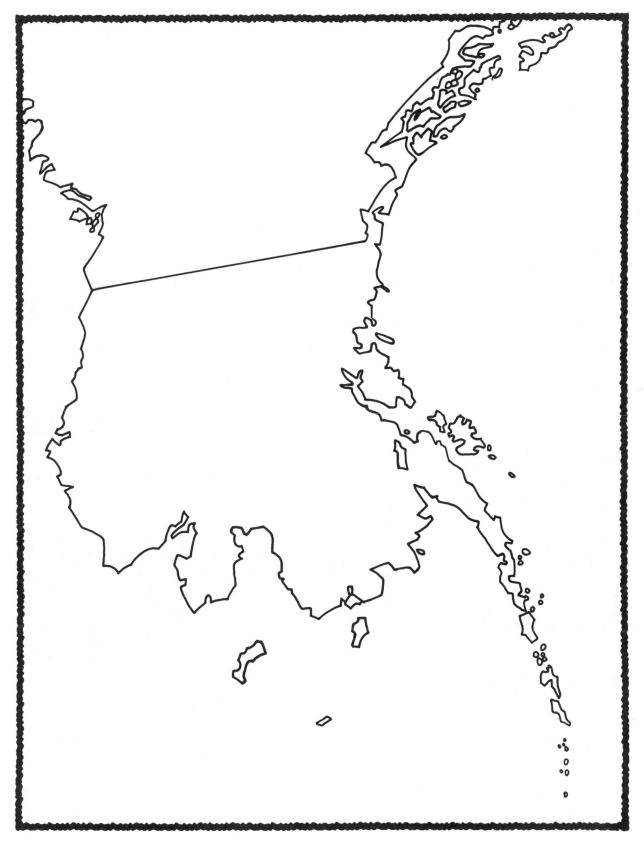

Native Alaskans

The native people of Alaska fall into two categories: the Arctic people and the remaining native people. The native people, generally thought of as "Indians," crossed the Bering Strait from Asia over a land bridge that no longer exists. They then spread across and down throughout North America. This migration may have begun as early as 50,000 B.C. The Arctic people, however, came by boat to North America from Siberia. This migration took place from about 3000 to 1000 B.C., long after the other groups had crossed the bridge.

The Arctic People of Alaska fall into two groups, Eskimo and Aleut. The name "Eskimo," meaning "Eaters of Raw Meat," was given to the Arctic people by the Algonquin Indians. Many of these people now prefer their original native names, Inuit in Canada and Inupiat (or Inupiaq) and Yu'pik in Alaska. The Aleuts are closely related to the Eskimos and traveled to Alaska from Siberia in boats. Their language is closely related to that of other Arctic cultures, and they also share many characteristics with the Northwest Indian groups. They live in the Aleutian Islands off the southwestern coast of Alaska. All of these Arctic people live in harsh winter climates along the Alaskan coast and are heavily dependent on the sea.

The rest of the native population falls into two categories: the Subarctic Athabascans and the Northwest Indians of the coastal area of southeastern Alaska. The Athabascans are divided into groups that live in many different locations. The Northwest Coast Indians of Alaska include the Tlingit, Haida, and Tsimshian. These native groups generally lived along the ocean's edge and used wood from the nearby giant forests for their homes and totem poles.

Members of these native groups hunted and fished for their food. Today, food can be purchased at grocery stores. Many Alaskan natives still hunt and fish part of the year, however, they now use rifles and shotguns instead of harpoons, spears, and bows and arrows. They have power-driven canvas canoes instead of kayaks and snowmobiles instead of dog sleds. Most live in frame house instead of igloos, hide tents, and wood, stone, and sod huts, and they use electricity, kerosene, or oil as fuel instead of animal fat. Wool, cotton, and synthetic clothing has largely replaced garments made from animal skins.

Name _____

The Tlingit Indians

The Tlingits, like other Northwest Indians, used wood to make their houses, totem poles, canoes, and chests. Some Tlingit bands made blankets from cedar-bark fiber and wool. The wool was dyed, and the blankets were woven into intricate designs. Like other Northwest Indians, Tlingits incorporated two major shapes into all of their designs, the "U" and the ovoid. These shapes were used to make abstract designs as well as animal designs.

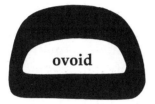

Use these two major shapes to design the Tlingit blanket below.

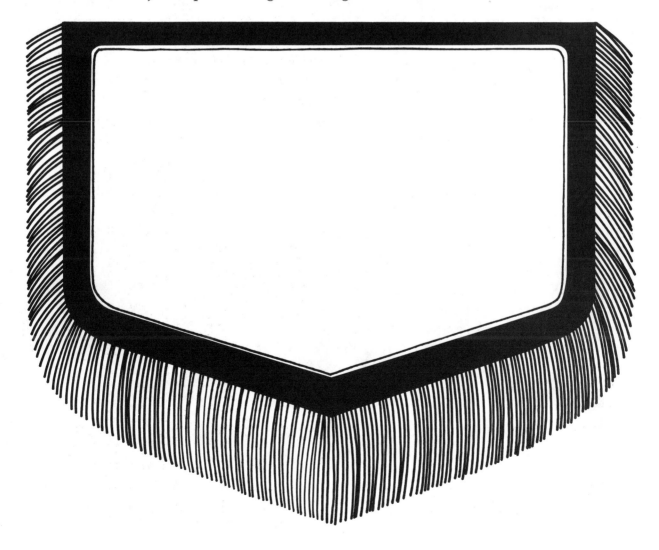

Name _____

Inupiat Carvings

The Inupiats used soapstone and walrus tusk ivory to make beautiful carvings. A carving was often a model of an Arctic animal or of the *inua*, or spirit, of the animal.

Draw an animal or the inua of an animal that you would like to carve. Keep the lines simple.

When you have completed your design, draw it carefully with a sharp pencil onto a bar of soap. Use a plastic knife or other carving tool to shave away the areas that are outside your design. Work slowly and carefully to avoid shaving off any parts of the design. When you are finished, polish your soap carving with a piece of soft cloth.

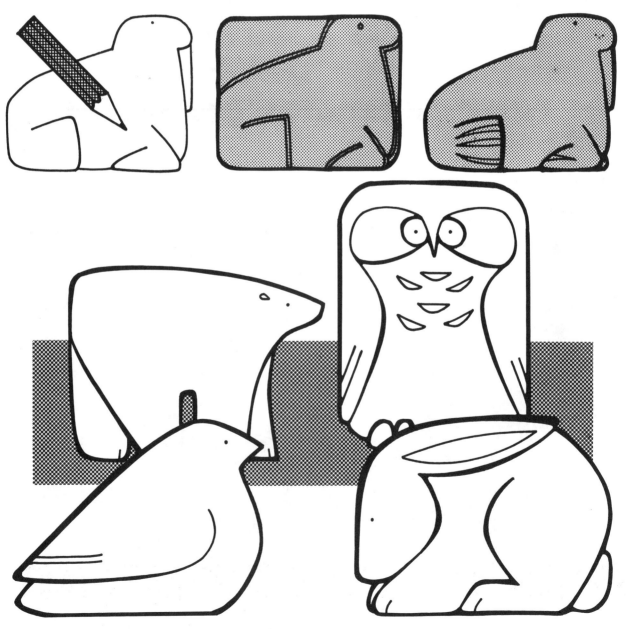

Name _____

Inupiat Language

Some words in the Inupiat language and their English translations are shown below.

aana	grandmother
aniu	snow
ataata	father
ava	grandfather
mazaq	sun
umiaq	large boat
uniat	dog sled
qimugun	dog

Write a story about the life of Inupiats in Alaska.
Include as many Inupiat words as you can.

_____

_____

_____

_____

_____

_____

_____

_____

_____

_____

_____

_____

_____

_____

mazaq aniu qimugun

Haida

The Haida were known as master woodcarvers. Like other Northwest Indians, they carved elaborate totem poles, often from giant redwoods. A totem pole told a story about the people and animals pictured on it. Some poles were memorials to dead family members. Other totem poles were part of decorative entries to homes, telling something about the families who lived there.

Animals that represented guardian spirits were common on the totem poles. These were carved using the basic ovoid and "U" shapes. Some of the most common animals used by the Haida are shown below.

raven

beaver

hawk

bear

Design a totem pole that would be appropriate to put outside your family's home. Use at least one of the traditional designs in your pole. When you are finished, explain why you chose this design.

Native People of Alaska

Alaska's natives belong to several distinct groups. Here are some examples:

Aleut
(A-loot)

The Aleuts settled in the Aleutian Islands about 2000 B.C. The word "Aleut" means "island." They lived mainly on animals of the sea, such as seals, sea otters, and whales, but also hunted caribou and bear. The Aleuts lived in communal houses up to 240 feet long. The majority of Aleuts now live on the mainland in protected native villages.

Athabascan
(Ath-a-bas'-ken)

The Athabascan Indians live in the interior of Alaska. They were originally divided into hunting bands, each with its own territory. These bands hunted moose, caribou, musk ox, and hare. The Athabascan language or related languages are spoken by Indians as far south as Mexico. The Navajo and Apache speak Athabascan languages, as well.

Haida
(Hī'-da)

The Haidas are found in southeastern Alaska. They mainly ate food from the sea, including sea otters, sea lions, and salmon. The Haida lived in large cedar houses that faced the sea, each with a totem pole at the entrance. Haidas were the most skilled maritime boat builders. Today few Haidas remain. A community of Haidas lives at Hydaburg on the southern end of Prince of Wales Island in Alaska.

**Inupiat
or Inupiaq**
(In-yoo'-pi-at)

The Inupiats migrated from Asia and spread across Canada. While today's Inupiats live in modern houses in northwestern coastal areas of Alaska, they still follow the "old ways" by hunting seal and walrus each year when the ice breaks up. Today there are bilingual schools where Inupiat children learn both English and their own language.

Tlingit
(Tling-git)

The Tlingits live in the southeastern area of Alaska known as the panhandle. Traditionally, they ate fish, deer, goat, bear, and rabbit. They were known as traders. Their homes were buildings made of cedar planks that housed several families. Along with the Haidas, the Tlingits have a reputation as being among the best Alaskan fishermen.

Yu'pik
(Yoo'-pik)

The Yu'piks settled on the western and southwestern coasts of Alaska. They were dependent on the sea for animals that provided food, materials for clothing, and other important products.

Native People of Alaska
(continued)

The map below shows the location of the native groups discussed on page 57.

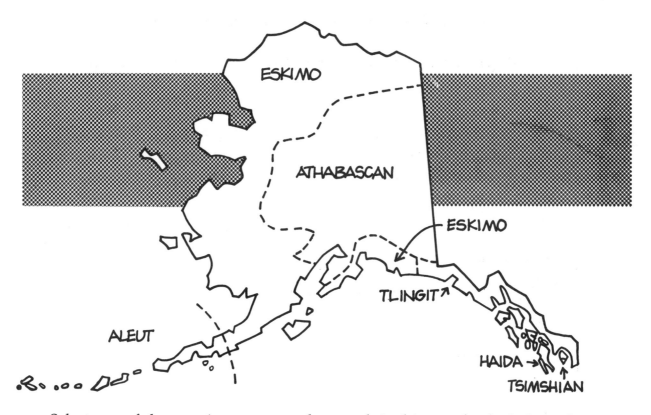

Select one of these native groups and research its history, food, clothing, housing, customs, folklore, and art. Create a diorama of a typical scene in a traditional community of this native group. Make your setting as accurate as possible.

Name _____

Amazing Arctic Animals

Without looking in a book, make a list of as many animals of the Arctic as you can. Include animals that were mentioned in books you have read about the Iditarod.

Choose one animal. Do research to determine the following information:

- physical description (What is it's color and approximate size and weight, etc.)
- habitat (Where does it live?)
- diet (What does it eat?)

When you have completed your report, design a three-dimensional zoo enclosure that duplicates the animal's natural habitat as closely as possible. Make a model of your animal to place in the enclosure. Then complete the sign below. Place it outside the enclosure to tell visitors about the animal.

name of animal: _____

☐ mammal ☐ bird ☐ fish ☐ other _____

habitat: _____

physical description: _____

diet: _____

fascinating facts: _____

_____

_____

Name _____

Dogs of the North Country

The rules of the Iditarod Trail Committee state that the dogs used in the Iditarod must be "northern breeds." These are dogs that are able to withstand the harsh northern climates.

List some dogs that you think are northern breeds.

Use reference books to check your guesses. Find as much information as you can in order to fill out the chart below.

breed of dog	average size	average weight	description of dog

Now decide which two breeds of dog you would prefer to have on your Iditarod team. Write your choices below, and explain how the special qualities of each breed you picked would help in a long sled race.

1. _____

_____

_____

2. _____

_____

_____

Name _____

Pack Your Bags for Alaska!

Design a travel brochure for Alaska. In your brochure, include information about the following:

- population
- climate in summer and winter
- major cities
- places of interest and historical sites
- natural resources
- native cultures
- wildlife
- any other interesting facts about the state

Create color drawings to make your brochure as attractive as possible.

Extended Social Studies and Research Activities

- Make a relief map of Alaska by mounting a map on cardboard. In a bowl, mix one cup of flour with one cup of salt and add water to make a dough. Use the dough to mold three-dimensional mountains on the map. Paint the entire map when it dries.

- Research **diphtheria**. Find out its causes, its symptoms, and how it is treated. Include information about why it is no longer a threat in our country.

- **Skijoring** is another sport that can involve dogs. Find out as much as you can about it and make a poster to illustrate the sport.

- Do a report on the gold rush in Alaska. Find out what life was like in the towns along the Iditarod trail that were involved in the gold rush.

- Research the part of Alaska's history known as "Seward's Folly." What was this event? Why was it called that? Write an editorial about Seward's Folly that might have appeared in a newspaper of that time.

- Make a three-dimensional model of the totem pole you designed on page 56 by using a paper-towel roll. Paint it when you are finished.

- Salmon were a vital resource to the Alaskan native and are important now as a major industry. Salmon have an interesting life cycle. Research this life cycle and illustrate it on a chart.

- Indians of southeastern Alaska held festive celebrations known as **potlatches**. Potlatch is a native slang word that comes from the word "patshatl" or "giving." The potlatch brought together guests from great distances in order to celebrate a special event. Often a totem pole was raised, and there was a large feast and gift giving. Compare the potlatch to a similar event in your family. What did the event celebrate? How was the celebration made special? Share your memories with the class.

Name _____

Extended Social Studies
and Research Activities
(continued)

Super Social Studies and Research Challenge

- The construction of the Alaskan pipeline caused a great deal of protest from environmentalists, who were concerned about its effect on Alaska's wildlife. Now there is discussion of exploring new oil fields, and the same concern has been voiced. Research this issue and prepare two arguments for and two against this new oil exploration. Hold a debate with a classmate.

- Compare the size and population of Alaska to those of your state. What conclusions can you draw from the differences in the numbers?

- Russia has had a strong influence on the history and culture of Alaska. Research this part of Alaskan history and find out what influences from Russian culture remain in Alaska.

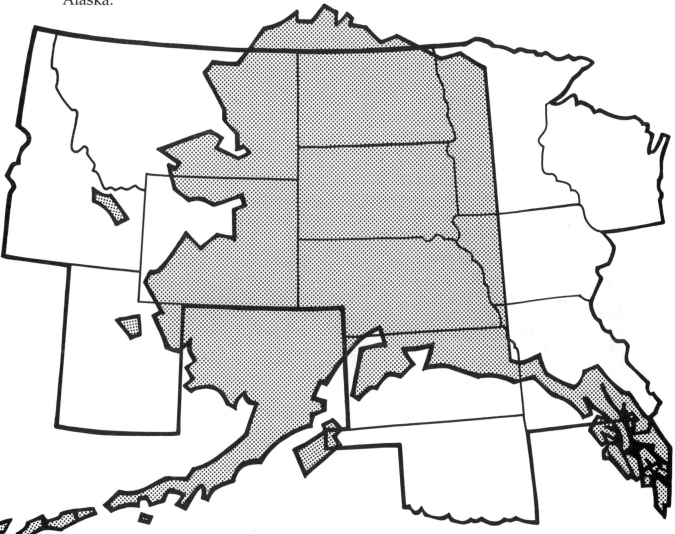

Name _____

Call Me Courageous

It takes great courage for a man or woman to run the Iditarod. There are many life-threatening risks at every turn—the intense cold, wildlife, storms, and equipment failure. Just to cross the finish line (regardless of what place a musher is in) is a triumph in personal strength.

Think of a time in your life when you were faced with a great challenge and acted with courage. Describe what happened and how you showed courage. Design a trophy for yourself commemorating that special event. Put your name on the trophy.

Name _____

Togo, the Forgotten Hero

A statue of Balto, the lead dog who brought the team carrying diphtheria serum into Nome, was placed in Central Park in New York. Leonhard Seppala was disappointed that his lead dog, Togo, did not receive the same recognition in spite of the fact that Togo led the team for 260 miles of the Serum Run.

In the space below, design a monument to honor Togo. When you are finished, tell where you would place the monument and why.

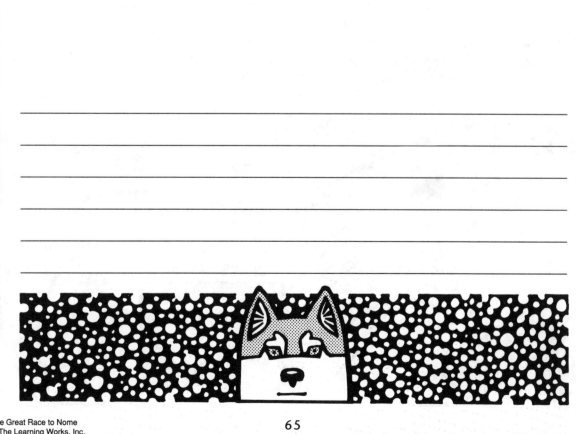

The Last Great Race Game

In the space on the next page, design a board for a game based on the Iditarod race. Use the following guidelines when planning your game:

1. Include accurate information about the Iditarod in your game. Include hazards, rules. and basic knowledge about the race and mushing. Your game should be designed for 2–4 players.

2. After you plan your board in the space on the next page, enlarge it and neatly copy it onto a piece of posterboard or cardboard. Use a ruler to make the lines and a stencil for the letters. Make all marks lightly in pencil, and then go over them with a marker. Make your board attractive by coloring it and adding illustrations.

3. Design your game pieces. Do a rough draft of everything before you make the final product. If you use questions, be sure to provide the answers with your game.

4. Include all game pieces. Put them in a plastic sandwich bag and attach it to the board with a paper clip.

5. Choose a name for your game. Be sure the name appears on the board.

6. Write the instructions to your game. Prepare a final copy that has been edited for spelling and punctuation errors. Fold and place these rules in your plastic game bag.

7. Play your game with some friends or family members to test it out. Check to see if the instructions are sufficiently clear so that everyone understands how to play the game without directions from you.

The Last Great Race Game
(continued)

Plan your game board in the box below.

_____
name of game

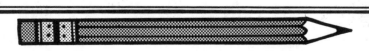

Name _____

Red Lanterns

The Red Lantern Award is given to the last musher to cross the finish line in Nome. Originally it was given as a joke because the last person was so far behind that he or she needed extra light. Now it represents an ability to "stick to it" in spite of all the odds and the musher's race position.

On a separate piece of paper, write a paragraph in which you speculate as to why the mushers complete the race even when it is obvious they will be among the last to finish. Then, write a paragraph describing a time when you showed persistence in spite of overwhelming obstacles.

Bibliography

Books about the Iditarod and dog sledding:

Cooper, Michael. *Racing Sled Dogs—An Original North American Sport*. Clarion Books, New York, 1988.

Crisman, Ruth. *Racing the Iditarod Trail*. Dillon Press, New York, 1983.

* Dolan, Ellen M. *Susan Butcher and the Iditarod Trail*. Walker Publishing, New York, 1993.

Dougherty, Jim. "A Legend Still Lives as Sled Dogs Race Across the Snows." *Smithsonian*, March, 1988.

* Gardiner, John Reynolds. *Stone Fox*. Harper & Row, New York, 1980.

* Gill, Shelley. *Kiana's Iditarod*. Paws IV, Homer, AK, 1992.

Iditarod Runner magazine. Iditarod Trail Committee, Wasilla, AK.

Mush With P.R.I.D.E.—Sled Dog Care Guidelines. Mush With P.R.I.D.E., 1993.

* O'Dell, Scott. *Black Star, Bright Dawn*. Houghton Mifflin, Boston, 1988.

* O'Neill, Catherine. *Dogs on Duty*. National Geographic Society, 1988.

* Paulsen, Gary. *Dogteam*. Delacorte Press, New York, 1993.

* Paulsen, Gary. *Woodsong*. Puffin Books, New York, 1990.

* Reit, Seymour. *Race Against Death*. Scholastic, New York, 1976.

* Riddles, Libby. *Danger, the Dog Yard Cat*. Paws IV. Homer, AK, 1989.

* Seibert, Patricia. *Mush!* Millbrook Press, Brookfield, CT, 1992.

Sherwonit, Bill. *Iditarod—The Great Race to Nome*. Alaska Northwest Books, Anchorage, 1991.

* Shields, Mary. *Can Dogs Talk?* Pyrola Publishing, Fairbanks, 1991.

* Shields, Mary. *Loving a Happy Dog*. Pyrola Publishing, Fairbanks, 1992.

* Shields, Mary. *Secret Messages: Training a Happy Dog*. Pyrola Publishing, Fairbanks, 1993.

Shields, Mary. *Sled Dog Trails*. Pyrola Publishing, Fairbanks, 1984.

* Standiford, Natalie. *The Bravest Dog Ever—The True Story of Balto*. Random House, New York, 1989.

Stout, Peg. *Alaska Women in the Iditarod*. State Education Agency, Alaska, 1992.

Books about native culture:

Beck, Mary L. *Heroes and Heroines—Tlingit-Haida Legends*. Alaska Northwest Books, Anchorage, 1985.

* Carlstrom, Nancy White. *Northern Lullaby*. Philomel Books, New York, 1992.

* Books written specifically for children.

Bibliography
(continued)

* Colene, Terri. *Ka-Ha-Si and the Loon—An Eskimo Legend*. Watermill Press, New Jersey, 1990.

* Ekoomiak, Normee. *Arctic Memories*. Henry Holt & Co., New York, 1988.

* "The Eskimos of Alaska." *Cobblestone*, November, 1985.

* Green, Paul. *I Am Eskimo—Aknik My Name*. Alaska Northwest Books, Anchorage, 1959.

Harris, Lorle K. *Tlingit Tales*. Naturegraph Publishing Co., Happy Camp, CA, 1985.

* Hoyt-Goldsmith, Diane. *Arctic Hunter*. Holiday House, New York, 1992.

* Kalman, Bobbie, and Belsey, William. *An Arctic Community*. Crabtree Publishing Co., New York, 1988.

* Kendall, Russ. *Eskimo Boy*. Scholastic, Inc., New York, 1992.

* McNutt, Nan. *The Bentwood Box*. Nan McNutt, Petersburg, AK, 1984.

* McNutt, Nan. *The Button Blanket*. Nan McNutt, Petersburg, AK, 1986.

Miles, Charles. *Indian and Eskimo Artifacts of North America*. Henry Regnery Co., Chicago, 1963.

* Osinski, Alice. *The Eskimo—The Inuit and Yupik People*. Childrens Press, Chicago, 1985.

* Rickman, David. *Northwest Coast Indians Coloring Book*. Dover Publications, New York, 1984.

* Rodgers, Jean. *Goodbye, My Island*. Greenwillow Books, New York, 1983.

* Robinson, Tom D. *An Eskimo Birthday*. Dodd, Mead, and Co., New York, 1975.

Waldman, Carl. *Encyclopedia of Native American Tribes*. Facts on File Publications, New York, 1988.

Wherry, Joseph H. *The Totem Pole Indians*. Wilfred Funk, Inc., New York, 1964.

Books about Alaska:

* Holen, Susan Dell. *Alaskan Wildlife—A Coloring Book*. Paisley Publishing, Anchorage, 1988.

The Alaska Almanac. Alaska Northwest Books, Anchorage, 1993.

* "Those Mysterious Lights in the Sky." *National Geographic WORLD*. December, 1987.

Understanding the Aurora. Geophysical Institute of the University of Alaska, Fairbanks.

* Books written specifically for children.

Clip Art

THE GREAT RACE

Answer Key

Tangram Designs (page 35):

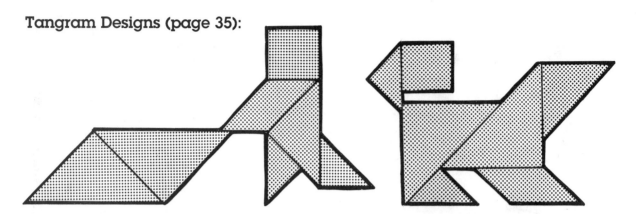

Math Challenges (page 38):

1. 156
2. 506
3. 214,942
4. Answer will vary according to the year
5. 35
6. $4,375
7. 72
8. 178
9. 687
10. 44

More Math Challenges (page 39):

1. 70
2. 39
3. 10:20 A.M.
4. 53 degrees (Don't forget zero!)
5. 116.1 (southern); 116.3 (northern)
6. 423 lbs.; 3 trips
7. A: 80 lbs.; B: 32 lbs.
8. $124,250
9. 214 hours
10. 6,030 lbs.; 60,300 lbs.

Sleds in Color (page 41):

The red sled belongs to Susan Butcher, the green sled belongs to Martin Buser, the blue sled belongs to Jeff King, and the purple sled belongs to Rick Swenson.

Sled Dogs in Line (page 42):

Mousey is fifth, Flopsey is fourth, Fidget is third, Jack is second, and Granite is first.

Musher Movers (page 43):

DeeDee Jonrowe is at McGrath, Susan Butcher is at Rohn Roadhouse, Martin Buser is at Nikolai, Jeff King is at Skwentna, and Joe Redington, Sr. is at Rainy Pass.